YOUR KNOWLEDGE HAS VALUE

- We will publish your bachelor's and master's thesis, essays and papers

- Your own eBook and book - sold worldwide in all relevant shops

- Earn money with each sale

Upload your text at www.GRIN.com and publish for free

Bibliographic information published by the German National Library:

The German National Library lists this publication in the National Bibliography; detailed bibliographic data are available on the Internet at http://dnb.dnb.de .

This book is copyright material and must not be copied, reproduced, transferred, distributed, leased, licensed or publicly performed or used in any way except as specifically permitted in writing by the publishers, as allowed under the terms and conditions under which it was purchased or as strictly permitted by applicable copyright law. Any unauthorized distribution or use of this text may be a direct infringement of the author s and publisher s rights and those responsible may be liable in law accordingly.

Imprint:

Copyright © 2016 GRIN Verlag
Print and binding: Books on Demand GmbH, Norderstedt Germany
ISBN: 9783668676046

This book at GRIN:

https://www.grin.com/document/418380

Kevin Dieterich

Aus der Reihe: e-fellows.net stipendiaten-wissen
e-fellows.net (Hrsg.)
Band 2728

The unconditional basic income as an approach to a solution of the precarization of labor

GRIN Verlag

GRIN - Your knowledge has value

Since its foundation in 1998, GRIN has specialized in publishing academic texts by students, college teachers and other academics as e-book and printed book. The website www.grin.com is an ideal platform for presenting term papers, final papers, scientific essays, dissertations and specialist books.

Visit us on the internet:

http://www.grin.com/

http://www.facebook.com/grincom

http://www.twitter.com/grin_com

Hochschule für Wirtschaft und Recht Berlin
- Berlin School of Economics and Law –

Department of Business and Economics
Bachelor Programme - International Business Management
400591 – Work, Business and Society

Summer semester 2016

The unconditional basic income
as an approach to a solution of the precarization of labor

Berlin, August 11, 2016

by Kevin Dieterich

Content

1. Introduction 2
2. The dangerous drift towards precarious working conditions 2
3. The idea of an unconditional basic income 4
4. The unconditional basic income debate 5
4.1. The unconditional basic income as an approach to fight precarity 5
4.2. Criticism of basic income models 6
5. Concluding reflections and alternative approaches 8
Reference List 9

1. Introduction

Our era of digitalization, interconnectivity and fast technological developments leads as a result to a continuously increasing degree of machine work per wage earner and thus similarly to ever-growing productivity increases. This development, to generate more output given the same time and unchanged input in manual labor is as such not to be assessed negative, but rather a desirable foundation of human progress. It is however problematic, that this tendency of productivity improvements under capitalistic production conditions threatens the existence of those wage-dependents that become victims of rationalisation efforts by firms, in other words, many workers run the risk that their workplaces will be eliminated due to technology. The absurdity is founded in the fact that the working population is producing the means on their own, by which they make themselves superfluos through self-created capital accumulation. Increases in productivity therefore do not lead to a situation where workers become incresingly work-free, but in fact become jobless and at the same time are being pushed into precarious employment relationships. But, due to the fact that the participation in social output - the consumption - is directly linked to job performance inputs, from which however a growing number of workers are excluded via rationalisation, only the portion of continuously employed people will gain from the rise in work productivity. The trend that the production of goods is becoming progressively independent from human work input, requires a political rethinking in which the employment system and allocation systems (of income and goods) are decoupled from each other. (Vobruba 2006, pp. 9–11) With a constant increase of individual wealth on the one hand and a constantly decreasing possibility to secure a minimum existence by the means of stable working contracts, a political redistribution of work, wealth and income is needed.

This necessity can be seen as the basis of the debate on the need of an unconditional basic income as a measure against the proceeding precarisation tendency of labor relations.

In what follows, I will address the emerging problem of precarious working conditions in Germany as a result of neoliberal capitalism (2). I will then introduce the concept of an unconditional basic income (3), before taking up the debate if a basic income could counteract the factors that lead to precarity by analyzing and comparing the statements of sociologists and representations of interests in that field (4). Finally, this paper will conclude by evaluating the aforementioned explanations and suggesting alternative approaches to the topical problem (5).

2. The dangerous drift towards precarious working conditions

In the recent decades, politicians all over the world took up ideas by neoliberal macroeconomists that see market development dependent on free competition and market deregulation. The consequence of this was that countries increased labor market flexibility and thereby decreased risks for the firms on the one hand, but shifted at the same time higher risks of unemployment and insecurity onto the working class, "[t]he result has been the creation of a global 'precariat', consisting of many millions around the world without an anchor of stability." (Standing 2011, p. 1)

Workers that find themselves in the „zone of precarity"[1] are subject to insecure, often low-paid and temporary or fixed-term employment relationships, that are expressed by short-term termination of employment contracts, and difficult social and living conditions. Notable is that the occurrence of this form of labor relationships is not only a phenomenon on the margin or which is taking place in developing countries only. In recent years, precarious working conditons are observable in the midst of the German society and comprises even well trained workers. Especially women in the service sector, interns and migrants run the risk of ending up in precarious jobs, leading as a result to frustrations, a feeling worthlessness and being disregarded by society (Dörre 2014, p. 79).

Especially migrants are hit hard by the precarious job market, for the one part as Standing explains, this group is being "demonised" and has to face accusations of being "criminals by nature, job thieves, being dirty and a potential disease risk" and thus are considered guilty until they can prove otherwise (Standing 2011, p. 146) and on the other they are victims of a particular precarity trap, as they emigrate from countries with a lower real wage and job expectations, making them more likely to accept precarious job offerings without prospects in the new host country. On top, hostility against migrants often enjoys broad societal support.[2] (Standing 2011, p. 114)

Before starting to evaluate how an unconditional income could be used to fight precarization, it is essential to identify the elements and variables that define precarity. Basically, any worker that lacks labor-related securities such as adequate *income*-earning opportunities on the labor market, *employment security* including dismissal protection and long-term contracts, *physical security* at the workplace as well as the opportunity to *gain further skills* and the possibility to be "heard" by some form of *representation*, finds himself in a precarious situation (Standing 2011, pp. 9–10; ILO - International Labour Organization n.d., p.1).

Above, the precariat is under continous pressure of time, owing to exhausting overtime hours and deadline pressures which put the workers under a constant feeling of being drained, which in turn lowers productivity and makes it harder to do creative work. (Standing 2011, pp. 130–131) In their jobs in turn, employees in precarious working relationship lack a work-based *identity* with their employer and long-term employees, meaning that the precariat does not feel part of a solidaristic labor community, this is due to the fact that they do not want to commit themselves to a job as a dismissal could be declared at any (Standing 2011, p. 12)

---

[1] Castel developed a model in which he divided societies into three distinct zones on the base of their labor market access and security – the protected "zone of integration", the growing "zone of precarity", which is subject of this paper and the "zone of detachment", to a large extent socially isolated and permantly excluded from the labor market (Dörre 2014, p. 75)

This blends seamlessly into the fact that the uncertainty of precarious working conditions is not providing possibilities to come up with a long-term life plan. (Dörre 2014, p. 75)

Our social security system that binds unemployment benefits on efforts of even taking lower rung jobs compared to the one maybe performed for years before, can result in a year-long destruction of the personal wage level for which the wage-earner worked for over the course of many years. The pressure to accept part-time positions (majoritarian women) has comparable impacts and the political initiative of transferring people out of unemployment into 'mini-jobs' may give the impression of low unemployment rates, but it is definitely not a solution against the precarization of labor. (Standing 2011, p. 15)

For the realisation of recovering real worker security in recent years, different unconditional basic income approaches have been developed.

3. The idea of an unconditional basic income

The aforementioned explanations have showed that precarization leads to an uneven distribution and access to economic security, time, information and purchasing power between members of a society. (Standing 2011, p. 171)

The unconditional basic income can thus be seen as an approach to fundamentally reform these existing conditions. The realization concepts how an unconditional basic income could be implemented vary dramatically especially between the political camps from which the approach is claimed[3]. However, all concepts have in common that they recommend an income, paid to members of a community based on three characteristics – individual claim (not a household claim), no proof of neediness and unconditionality of entitlement to payments (not linked to gainful employment). (Spannagel 2015, p. 7) Additionally, the recipients of such a payment should not be limited in the choice of their expenditures, so that the income is non-paternalistic. (Standing 2011, pp. 171–173)

Two models that gained particular attention in the public debate in Germany and which can be seen as the most mature proposals so far are the basic income model by Götz Werner, founder of the drugstore chain "dm", and the solidary citizen's income, an idea by Dieter Althaus, German politician of the Christian Democratic Union.

Werners pursues with his model the goal of strengthening the "self-realization" of citizens, meaning to liberate the current constraint of ensuring one's existence via gainful work and to promote the creative development of the personality. Technically, Werner proposes to eliminate the income tax and all social security contributions and in turn to finance the basic income by a consumption tax of up to 50 %. (Spannagel 2015, p. 6; Werner & Goehler 2010, p. 241 ff.)

---

[3] Support for such a concept can be found from individuals of almost all political directions, naming Dieter Althaus ("CDU"), Katja Kipping ("Die Linke"), the liberal party "FDP" and the youth organization of "die Grünen" as only a few examples from the German discourse. Globally, the association BIEN (Basic Income Earth Network) is committed to promote the idea of a basic income.

Althaus on the contrary aims with his model to radically simplify the current tax- and transfer system and to further flexibilize and deregulate the labor market. The solidary citizen's income should function as a negative income tax with a basic income contribution level based on the earned income. On top, Althaus plans to grant additional transfer payments based upon neediness. Contrary to Werners' model, this basic income is not intended to ensure livelihood security. To fund the concept, Althaus recommends a mixed financing based on the pillars of a consumption tax, a payroll tax by wage earners and a "flat" income tax, with a standardized tax rate without differentiations on the wage level. (Spannagel 2015, pp. 6–7)

4. The unconditional basic income debate

Whether the implementation of a basic income is regarded to be useful to fight precarious working conditions is a topic of heated discussion not only between politics, sociologists and macroeconomists, but also in the broad public debate.

In the following, I will exemplary point out the prevailing opposing views on the topic primarily by two mutually contradictory explanations on the implications of basic income models for the precariat by the sociologists, Guy Standing, British research professor at the University of London and co-founder of the Basic Income Earth Network (Standing n.d.), and Christoph Butterwegge, basic income opponent and German professor of political science at the University of Cologne (Butterwegge n.d.).

4.1. The unconditional basic income as an approach to fight precarity

"The precariat is not victim, villain or hero – it is just a lot of us."
- Guy Standing (Standing 2011, p. 183)

The freedom to say "no" to meaningless and low-paid work has only the individual, whose minimum subsistence level is guaranteed and a basic income would incrase this freedom of choice, explains Götz Werner is his work on a practical implementation of an unconditional basic income. As a result, workers would gain the opportunity to seek out job opportunities that offer superior securities, higher standards of living and that meet personal preferences. (Werner & Goehler 2010, p. 62)

The precariat is concerned with multiple aspects of uncertainty, one of their main anxieties they suffer from is the economic dimension of a job loss and the falling into the "zone of detachment". It is scientifically proven, that chronic financial insecurity produces stress and lowers the possibility to concentrate on work assignments, states Standing, referring to studies on chronic stress performed by Evans and Schamberg, and adds that therefore there should be a moral obligation to assure at least some basic economic security inpendent from individual discretion on acute neediness. According to him, such an elemantary security would make it easier for people in precarious situations to economically and psychologically cope with the uncertainty of labor relations and provide a reasonable basis on which individuals could "recover" from sudden negative changes related to working contracts. On this matter, he underlines the importance that basic social protection, which he regards to be an "almost universal human need and a worthy goal", should not be made conditional on some form of behavior or actually provided performance, because "if certain behaviour is unacceptable, it should be made a matter of law [...]. Linking social protection to conditionality is to bypass law, which is supposedly the same for all." (Standing, 2011, pp. 175) In this light, we can see an unconditional basic income as a method to diminish monetary insecurity differences between the zone of integration and the precariat, as it would function as an economic stabilizer and above reduce inequalities.

Macroeconomically seen, Standing argues that the provision of basic security via a basic income would simplify the present social security system, both for the state and the dependent persons, by consolidating and substituting the current transfer services and be characterized by higher efficiency than standard fiscal policy, due to a lower deadweight loss. (Standing, 2011, pp. 173–176)

Even though a basic income would reinforce the employment fluctuation and flexibility on the labor market, typically an indicator for precarious working conditions, by means of the financial support, job changes would then take place in environments of greater security and without financial pressure.

On the hand, says Standing, a basic income increases the ability accept low wages, as it supplements the income, on the other, it provides the possibility to bargain more strongly with the potential employer, due to the fact that one is not reliant on the one single job offer at hand. (Standing 2011, p. 178)

Current social policies only adequately reward labor in the traditional sense and punish individuals that do not or participate less in paid labor or engage in alternative work forms, such as in community services. As explained in the introduction, these policies neglect the development that in the future there will be not enough labor for "everyone". (Vobruba 2006, pp. 9–11) A basic income would counter the pressure to labor and increase capacities to engage outside the market. This leads also to the "time" aspect of basic income models. Standing sees the basic income as an option to recover individual control over time, needed make rational decisions. The precariat is "caught in trap", where they have to spent a growing amount of time into wage labor with diminishing returns to the same, which leads to exhaustion and in turn to an inability to grasp information needed to make reasonable judgements. (Standing 2011, p. 178)

4.2. Criticism of basic income models

„Some utopias are dangerous, because they distract from the search of more realistic alternatives."

- Castel and Tillmann (Castel & Tillmann 2007, p. 113)

Unlike Standing, Butterwegge exercises heavy criticism of unconditional income models, as in his opinion such an approach would be misleading to solve significant questions concerning precarious working conditions, because it would not change the distribution of wealth and harmonises with neo-liberal policies (Butterwegge 2016, para. 1). Contrary to expectations, a welfare policy based on a principle of giving everybody an equal share of the budget instead of granting individual social transfers based on neediness, would only lead to even greater inequalities, because it disadvantages individuals in difficult situations. (Butterwegge 2012, p. 424)

Kreutz sees the problem here, that the unconditional basic income shifts the responsibility for the existential security of the individual from the salary system to the state and by this withdraws the obligation of firms to pay workers adequate livelihood wages. Recipients of a basic income would accept even lower wages, by what firms could lower their workforce expenses and increase profits. (Kreutz 2010, p. 68)

The summarization of all (or most) current transfer payments into one single basic income, would not only play into the hands of neo-liberals by creating a "minimal state", to the precariats' perception it pretends to be beneficial. In this context, Butterwegge criticizes Werner for planning to abolish taxes on capital and profits and to fund his model by a dramatically increase of the VAT, even though exactly this tax hits low-income earners hardest.

Consequently, of the introduction of a basic income the relative poverty in a society would not change significantly and rather just shift risk of poverty threshold higher so that compulsory labor persists.

Likewise, the proposed systems would not change the distribution of wealth and actually rather worsen the gap between rich and poor as they plan to increase or levy taxes on earnings and wealth. (Butterwegge 2016, para. 2) In this respect, Butterwegge supports Heiner Flassbeck[4], who says that primarily high earners would profit from an unconditional basic income that are not in need of additional benefits for their livelihood, but if a basic income would be linked to precarious income conditions it would lack unconditionality. (Butterwegge 2012, p. 426)

The precariat would also suffer from an undermining of the labor market if a basic income is implemented. The persisting pressure to work for the previously mentioned reasons would force workers to accept any job without an option, thereby reinforce precarious working conditions and destroy reintegration possibilities into stable employment relationships. (Castel & Tillmann 2007, pp. 111–113) Particularly women could be pushed out of the labour market by an unconditional basic income fears Spannagel, researcher at the Institute of Economic and Social Research (WSI) within the Hans-Böckler-Foundation. She assumes that women receiving an unconditional basic income may quit their jobs and "fall back" into domestic work, may it be voluntary or forced. Simultaneously,

---

[4] Heiner Flassbeck (*1950) German economist and Chief of Macroeconomics and Development of the United Nations Conference on Trade and Development (UNCTAD) until 2012

employers could use the basic income as an argument not to deal with the reconciliation of work and family life. (Spannagel 2015, p. 13)

The main points of Butterwegge's criticism also focus on the solidary citizen's income by Althaus, describing it to be a "political bluff package". The consolidation of transfer payments into a lump sum, would in total only decrease the level of security of dependent individuals. Above the citizen's income increases wage flexibility and is directed against minimum wages, leading in turn to a publically accepted expansion of precarious work. Dismissal Protection, collective wage agreements and influence of labor unions would diminish, what seems to be the end of precariat's misery sees Butterwegge in reality as a paradise for companies that aggravates the precarious working situation. (Butterwegge 2012, p. 425)

5. Concluding reflections and alternative approaches

The conclusion can thus be drawn that those unconditional basic income proposals that aim to improve precarious employment relationships are noble, however, the two most mature concepts by Althaus and Werner can be assigned into the neoliberal discourse and as such would in many respects rather serve enterprises than to improve the situation of the precariat. Social transfers would be replaced, labor market further flexibilized and deregulated and dismissial protections laws loosen. (Spannagel 2015, p. 9)

The discussion revealed that extensive reforms are needed, nonetheless. It is therefore important to expand and reorganise social security system so that the Precariat is able to regain stability and becomes poverty-proof. (Butterwegge 2012, p. 427)

But Butterwegge does not only criticize exising basic income models, he also suggests a paradigm shift in the discourse to more sustainable measures and proposes in this matter a solidarity-based citizen's insurance scheme. This concept would incorporate also groups of workers that are not subject to social contributions[5] and abolish the contribution assessment ceiling to expand social security financial endowments for the one part and a levy on the value added[6] replacing the current social insurance contributions by firms.

Such an approach would disconnect the funding of the social system from the wages which are under increased pressure and thereby provide a higher degree of justice and social balance than a basic income and thus would be truly in the interest of the precariat and not only delude caring for the precariat's well-being. (Butterwegge 2016, para. 5)

---

[5] such as self-employed and civil servants
[6] contrary to the current social security contribution system, a levy on the value added ("Wertschöpfungsabgabe") would impose the social contributions by firms based on the level of gross value added instead of worker's gross wages and thereby aims to reach positive employment effects

Reference List

BUTTERWEGGE, C., n.d. *Vita*. Available at: <http://www.christophbutterwegge.de/vita.php> [Accessed 7 August 2016]

BUTTERWEGGE, C., 2012. *Krise und Zukunft des Sozialstaates*. 4., überarbeitete und erweiterte Auflage. Wiesbaden: VS Verlag für Sozialwissenschaften / Springer Fachmedien Wiesbaden GmbH Wiesbaden

BUTTERWEGGE, C., 2016. *Das Grundeinkommen, eine gefährliche Utopie*. OXI-Blog. Available at: <https://oxiblog.de/eine-gefaehrliche-utopie/> [Accessed 5 August 2016]

CASTEL, R., and TILLMANN, M., 2007. *Die Stärkung des Sozialen. Leben im neuen Wohlfahrtsstaat*. 2. Aufl. Hamburg: Hamburger Ed

DÖRRE, K., 2014. Precarity and Social Disintegration: A Relational Concept. *Journal für Entwicklungspolitik 4/2014. Capitalist Peripheries: Perspectives on Precarisation from the Global South and North*. Wien: Mattersburger Kreis für Entwicklungspolitik (Journal für Entwicklungspolitik (JEP); 4/2014)

ILO - INTERNATIONAL LABOUR ORGANIZATION, n.d. *Definitions: What we mean when we say "economic security"*. ILO - International Labour Organization. Available at: <http://www.ilo.org/public/english/protection/ses/download/docs/definition.pdf> [Accessed 7 August 2016]

KREUTZ, D., 2010. Bedingungslose Freiheit? Warum die Grundeinkommensdebatte den Freunden des Kapitalismus in die Hände spielt. *Blätter für deutsche und internationale Politik*(04), 65–77

SPANNAGEL, D., 2015. *Das bedingungslose Grundeinkommen: Chancen und Risiken einer Entkoppelung von Einkommen und Arbeit*. Düsseldorf. (WSI Report; 24/2014)

STANDING, G., n.d. *Résumé*. Available at: <http://www.guystanding.com/resume> [Accessed 7 August 2016]

STANDING, G., 2011. *The precariat. The new dangerous class*. London: Bloomsbury Academic

VOBRUBA, G., 2006. *Entkoppelung von Arbeit und Einkommen. Das Grundeinkommen in der Arbeitsgesellschaft*. Wiesbaden: VS Verlag für Sozialwissenschaften / GWV Fachverlage GmbH Wiesbaden

WERNER, G., and GOEHLER, A., 2010. *1.000 Euro für jeden. Freiheit, Gleichheit, Grundeinkommen*. 3. Aufl. Berlin

YOUR KNOWLEDGE HAS VALUE

- We will publish your bachelor's and master's thesis, essays and papers

- Your own eBook and book - sold worldwide in all relevant shops

- Earn money with each sale

Upload your text at www.GRIN.com
and publish for free